A Note From Rick Renner

I am on a personal quest to see a "revival of the Bible" so people can establish their lives on a firm foundation that will stand strong and endure the test when the end-time storm winds begin to intensify.

In order to experience a revival of the Bible in your personal life, it is important to take time each day to read, receive, and apply its truths to your life. James tells us that if we will continue in the perfect law of liberty — refusing to be forgetful hearers but determined to be doers — we will be blessed in our ways. As you watch or listen to the programs in this series and work through this corresponding study guide, I trust that you will search the Scriptures and allow the Holy Spirit to help you hear something new from God's Word that applies specifically to your life. I encourage you to be a doer of the Word that He reveals to you. Whatever the cost, I assure you — it will be worth it.

> Thy words were found, and I did eat them;
> and thy word was unto me the joy and rejoicing of mine heart:
> for I am called by thy name, O Lord God of hosts.
> — Jeremiah 15:16

Your brother and friend in Jesus Christ,

Rick Renner

Knowing the Will of God

Copyright © 2020 by Rick Renner
8316 E. 73rd St.
Tulsa, Oklahoma 74133

Published by Rick Renner Ministries
www.renner.org

ISBN 13: 978-1-68031-609-4

eBook ISBN 13: 978-1-68031-647-6

How To Use This Study Guide

This 5-lesson study guide corresponds to *"Knowing the Will of God" With Rick Renner* (Renner TV). Each lesson in this study guide covers a topic that is addressed during the program series, with questions and references supplied to draw you deeper into your own private study of the Scriptures on this subject.

To derive the most benefit from this study guide, consider the following:

First, it is recommended that you watch or listen to the program prior to working through the corresponding lesson in this guide. (Programs can also be viewed at **renner.org** by clicking on the Media/Archive links.)

Second, take the time to look up the scriptures included in each lesson. Prayerfully consider their application to your own life.

Third, use a journal or notebook to make note of your answers to each lesson's Study Questions and Practical Application challenges.

Fourth, invest specific time in prayer and in the Word of God to consult with the Holy Spirit. Write down the scriptures or insights He reveals to you about being filled with the Spirit and empowered by Him in your daily life.

Finally, take action! Whatever the Lord tells you to do according to His Word, do it.

For added insights on this subject, we are offering Rick Renner's book *The Will of God — the Key to Your Success.* You can also select from Rick's other available resources by placing your order at **renner.org** or by calling 1-800-742-5593.

TOPIC
Officially Dedicating Your Life To Do God's Will

SCRIPTURES

1. **Hebrews 10:7** — Then said I, Lo, I come (in the volume of the book it is written of me,) to do thy will, O God.
2. **Matthew 16:25** — For whosoever will save his life shall lose it: and whosoever will lose his life for my sake shall find it.
3. **Romans 12:1** — I beseech you therefore, brethren, by the mercies of God, that ye present your bodies a living sacrifice, holy, acceptable unto God, which is your reasonable service
4. **Luke 2:22** — And when the days of her purification according to the law of Moses were accomplished, they brought him to Jerusalem, to present him to the Lord.

GREEK WORDS

1. "servant" — **δοῦλος** (*doulos*): one completely surrendered to do the will of his master; one who forfeits his own will entirely, laying it aside forever, and lives to faithfully fulfill the will of his master; one who is perpetually bound to do the bidding of his owner; one whose principal task is to fulfill the desires of his master for the rest of his life; to help, assist, and fulfill his master's wants and dreams to the exclusion of all else; one whose existence is to service his master in whatever way the master asked or demanded; one whose will is completely swallowed up in the will of another
2. "beseech" — **παρακαλέω** (*parakaleo*): to urge, beseech, plead, beg, pray; pictures someone who has come closely alongside another person for the sake of speaking to him, consoling him, comforting him, or assisting him with instruction, counsel, or advice; depicts military leaders who came alongside their troops to urge, exhort, beseech, beg, and plead with them to stand tall and face their battles bravely; to earnestly beg; denotes a word of prayer

3. "mercies" — οἰκτιρμός (*oiktirmos*): tender feelings; compassion; a divine power released to help us

4. "present" — παρίστημι (*paristemi*): to place at one's disposal; to surrender; to offer as a sacrifice to God; to present as a special offering to God; to dedicate; used in Luke 2:22 to describe the moment when Joseph and Mary presented Jesus to God and dedicated Him in the Temple; to fully dedicate with no intention of ever taking back again

SYNOPSIS

Have you ever wondered about God's will for your life? Have you ever wondered how to find His perfect plan, will, and purpose and whether your life is in perfect alignment with it?

In this five-part series, **Knowing the Will of God**, you will learn how to know His will, as well as ways to confirm you are walking in His plan for your life. The following topics will be explored:

1. Officially Dedicating Your Life To Do God's Will
2. What Does 'Holy and Acceptable Unto God' Mean?
3. What Is Real Inward and Outward Transformation?
4. What Is the Good, Acceptable, and Perfect Will of God?
5. Six Signals To Know the Will of God

The emphasis of this lesson:

In Romans 12:1, Paul states that before you can ever know the will of God, you must first present your body as a living sacrifice to God. What does that mean? That is the topic of this lesson.

Knowing the Will of God

In this program, Rick states, "Over the years I have received thousands of letters from people wanting to know the will of God for their lives. When I began teaching on television many years ago, I encouraged those watching to write in. I said, 'If you need to know the will of God, write in, and we will answer your letter.' I was quite stunned by the response we received. In fact, so many people wrote, we quit counting the number of pieces of mail and began counting the mail by *the tons*. We were inundated with letters. Many wrote questions about healing or finances, but the number one question on people's hearts and minds was this: 'Can you please tell me, Brother Rick, what is God's plan for my life and how can I know it?'"

Many people struggle trying to discern God's will for their lives.

- *God, is this Your plan?*
- *Do You want me to marry this person?*
- *Am I supposed to take that job?*
- *What church am I supposed to attend?*

Many struggle to know God's plan for their lives. But here is the good news — it is possible to know God's precise plan for your life if you will fulfill the requirements in His Word. One thing is certain, you will never know the will of God if you are following your own will. As long as you have your own plan, your own ideas that you are hoping God's plan matches, you will probably never find the will of God. You must be willing to release your own plans and ideas and surrender them. "Surrendering" your own plans means to lay them aside so you can hear what God has to say. You must make the determination that God's Word, God's Voice, God's Spirit will be the dominating voice in your life; not your ideas, plans, or feelings. You have to lay all that aside and say, "God, I want to know Your Word, Your Voice; I want to hear what Your Spirit is saying. I am willing to lay all my plans aside so I can hear what You have to say to me." But as long as you are holding on to your own ideas, it will confuse things and make it more difficult for you to hear what God really wants to reveal to you.

'I Come To Do Thy Will'

The first step in finding God's will is you must be willing to release your own plans, release your own will, to hear the will of God. God's Voice, God's Word, and God's Spirit must be the dominating voice.

Hebrews 10:7 is a prophetic verse describing Jesus before He came to the earth.

> **Then said I, Lo, I come (in the volume of the book it is written of me,) to do thy will, O God.**

Jesus came with one explicit purpose: to do the exact will of the Father. But even Jesus had a moment when He struggled with the will of God. In the garden of Gethsemane, Jesus prayed three times, "Not *My* will, but *Thy* will be done." The Bible tells us Jesus was in agony while He prayed in the garden. The word "agony" is from the Greek word *agonia*. It is an athletic term describing two wrestlers hurling each other to the mat, one trying to gain the superiority over the other. The Bible says Jesus was in agony. His spirit knew the will of God; His mind did not want to do it. Who would want to go to the cross and to the grave? Jesus struggled. He was in agony; there was a wrestling match on the inside of Him. Three times, Jesus cried, "Not My will, but Thy will be done." Jesus was turning away from His own desires to surrender to the will of God.

Jesus was born to do the will of God, and He was single-minded about that fact. His focus was to do the will of God, without distractions, and He would not allow any other influence to sway Him or lead Him off track.

In order to stay focused and to know the will of God, you must first lay your own will aside. This is paramount to knowing the will of God. In order to hear what God wants to do with your life, His Voice, His Spirit, and His Word must be the dominating factor in your mind, in your emotions, and in your thinking.

You must be willing to really hear what God has to say.

Are You a Servant?

We all must ask ourselves the question: *Am I a servant?* The word "servant" is used throughout the New Testament to describe men and women who were surrendered to God's plan. The word "servant" in Greek is the word *doulos*. Some people say, "Well, I'm not a servant; I'm a son." Of course, you are a son, but you are also a servant. Paul, James, and Peter all used this word to describe themselves. They called themselves servants, the Greek word *doulos*.

The word *doulos* describes *one completely surrendered to do the will of his master*. If you are a servant of God, you are completely surrendered to do the will of your Master. A servant is one who forfeits His own will entirely, laying it aside forever, and lives to faithfully fulfill the will of his Master. A servant is one who is perpetually bound to do the bidding of his owner, one whose principal task in life — not secondary, but principal — is to fulfill the desires of his master for the rest of his life to help, assist, and fulfill his master's wants and dreams to the exclusion of all else. This word for "servant" describes one whose will is completely swallowed up in the will of another.

When you say that you are a servant of God, you are literally saying that your will has been swallowed up in the will of God. You have forfeited your own rights and plans, and now you are living exclusively to do the will of God above all else. The Bible calls each one of us servants of God, which means we are not here to do our own bidding; we are here to do the bidding of our Master. We are commissioned to do the will of God.

But again, to do the will of God you must first hear it. And you will never explicitly hear it until you decide that God's Voice, God's Word, and God's Spirit will be the dominating voice in your life. Then you must choose to live to do what He says — to obey His commands and to follow His directions. In effect, you must adopt the mindset that life is not about you!

Rick also related that he tells Denise and his family frequently, "This is not about us; we are not here for us. We were brought into this world to fulfill a purpose."

If You Are Under Heaven, You Have a Purpose

You might say, "Well, of course, God has a plan for the Renners. But does He really have a special, mapped-out plan for *me*?" Ecclesiastes 3:1 says, "To every thing there is a season, and a time to every purpose under the heaven."

If you are "under the heaven," you have a purpose! You did not come into this world accidentally. *You are not an accident!* In fact, before the first layer of the earth's crust was ever put into place, God already had a plan designed for you.

God has a plan for you. You are not in charge of coming up with a plan; it is not being created as you walk along in life. It was already made for you, and God is waiting for you to step into that marvelous plan. But as long as your own plans and ideas are more important to you than God's, you are never going to find the plan of God.

In order to find the plan of God, you must lay everything else aside in terms of your own plans and ideas for your life. You must forfeit it all and say, "God, my ears are open and my heart is open to hear only what

You have to say. I want Your Voice, Your Word, and Your Spirit to be the dominating voice in my life. I want to hear *Your* plan for me."

When you have a heart that is truly surrendered, you will begin to discover God's explicit plan for your life. Everything else has to be viewed as an unnecessary opinion, including your feelings and any of your previous plans.

Those who truly dedicate themselves to knowing God's plan to the level I'm describing will be those who actually find God's will for their lives.

Whoever Loses His Life Will Find It

In Matthew 16:25, Jesus made this amazing statement: "For whoever desires to save his life will lose it, but whoever loses his life for My sake will find it."

According to Jesus, if you hold on to your will and hang on to your plans and to everything *you* want to do — if you're just clinging to your own life — eventually you will "lose" it. You will lose out all around by holding on just to what *you* want and what *you* think is best for your life. But if you are willing to lose yourself for Jesus' sake, you will "find" your life, and what a thrilling life it will be! There is a marvelous discovery that takes place when you completely surrender yourself into the hands of Jesus.

In this segment, Rick related the following story:

> When I was younger, before we moved to the Soviet Union, I had my own plans. I thought I knew what I would be doing with my life. Our ministry was being blessed. I was writing books, and people were purchasing my books. Denise and I were living in a great season. I was conducting more than 400 meetings each year, and I believed I would build a large ministry in the United States. But suddenly, God spoke to me and said, "I want you to relocate your family to the Soviet Union." It wasn't even Russia at that time — it was the Soviet Union! But I knew I had heard His voice.
>
> The night God spoke to me concerning the Soviet Union was such a night of agony for me. That is the reason I can understand a little of what Jesus was experiencing in the garden of Geth-semane. There was such a wrestling matching going on inside me because God was telling me one thing while my mind was

saying, *What will happen to you if you do what God is telling you to do?* There was a fear factor while my heart was trying to trust the Lord. I wanted to do what God said, yet my soul was arguing against what God had spoken to me.

That night, I spent the entire night literally hugging the toilet, vomiting, because I was in such turmoil inside. God wasn't the reason I was vomiting. God didn't make me sick; it was my soul struggling with what He had said to me. It was my coming to a place of surrender. Why? Because I already had my plans. I thought I knew what I would be doing with the next years of my life. Then, suddenly, I heard the dominating voice of God telling me something very different that I had never considered. It was so explicit and clear that I knew it was God speaking to me. So the wrestling match had begun. But by morning, I had finally surrendered my soul. Again, Jesus said, if you lose your life for His sake, you will find it. And I "found" my life that night.

When I look back at what has happened since I surrendered my will completely to the Lord's will, I am so glad I didn't keep my family in the United States! It looked like we were leaving everything, but, in fact, when you step into the will of God, you step out of a black and white world into a full-color spectrum. We stepped into the book of Acts, and we have seen with our own eyes the power of God in operation. Our sons grew up with a worldview, speaking multiple languages with experiences they would have never had if we had remained in Tulsa, Oklahoma. So we lost nothing by obeying God's unique instructions and plans for our lives and following Him.

Jesus said, "If you lose your life for My sake, you will find it." That's why you must put away fear. Fear says, *Don't turn loose of your own plans; don't let go. This is YOUR life. What will happen to you if you obey the Lord?* But if you choose to lose your life for His sake — if you will get into alignment with God's plan for you — you will step into an amazing, abundant life. That is just a fact!

Paul's Urgent Call

Romans 12:1 and 2 is one of the most powerful passages in the Bible about knowing the will of God. Paul says to his reader *and to us*, "I beseech you therefore, brethren, by the mercies of God, that you present your bodies a living sacrifice, holy acceptable to God, which is your reasonable service" (*NKJV*).

In this verse Paul says, "I *beseech* you..." The word "beseech" is the Greek word *parakaleo*. The word *para* means *to be alongside*, and the word *kaleo* means *to call out to*. When these two words are compounded, the new word means *to urge someone very closely; to come alongside him; to beseech that individual; to plead, to beg, or to pray*. This could be translated, *"I pray you, I beseech you, I beg you."* Paul was calling out to them urgently. The same word *parakaleo* pictures *someone who has come closely alongside another person for the sake of speaking to him, consoling him, comforting him, or assisting him with instruction, counsel, or advice*. The same word was used to depict military leaders who came alongside their troops *to urge, exhort, beseech, beg and plead with them to stand tall to face their battles bravely*.

This Greek word also means *to earnestly beg*; it is a word for *prayer*. One scholar says that when Paul said, "I beseech you," it was a picture of Paul on his knees. He had dropped to his knees, saying, "I beseech you [*parakaleo*] — I'm coming alongside of you; I'm coming as close as I can get; and I'm pleading with and calling out to you. I am begging you." And because it is also a military term, this word "beseech" means Paul knew he was going to ask them to do something that would require warfare. Paul exhorts them, "Face this bravely; you can do it!" He was praying with them to do something, and he was telling them to conquer their flesh and to wage warfare against their own will.

The Mercies of God

Paul continued: "I beseech you therefore, brethren by the *mercies* of God..." Even the word "mercies" is important. It describes the tender feelings of God, the compassion of God — but, specifically, it is a divine power released to help us. Paul appealed to them and to believers everywhere today, "If you will do what I am telling you to do, God will release His mercy to enable you to do this." But what is it that we are to do? We are to present our bodies a living sacrifice, holy, acceptable unto God, which is our reasonable service (Romans 12:1).

The word "present" is the Greek word *paristemi*. It means *to place at one's disposal*. When Paul said to present your bodies, He was saying, "Present your body to be at God's disposal." Simply put, Paul was exhorting us to surrender our lives to God. We are to offer a sacrifice of our lives to God as a special offering to Him. It also means *to dedicate*.

No Turning Back

The same word is used in Luke 2: 22, which says, "When the days of Mary's purification according to the law of Moses were accomplished, they brought Jesus to Jerusalem to present him unto the Lord." That word "present" is the same Greek word found in Romans 12:1. It means *to fully dedicate with no intention of every taking it back again*. When Joseph and Mary presented Jesus, they permanently presented Him and officially dedicated Him with no intention of ever taking Him back again. Now Paul uses the same word to express that if you want to know the will of God, you must first present yourself as a living sacrifice; officially dedicate yourself — your body, your mind, your emotions, your spirit — to God *officially, permanently, forever, with no intention to ever take yourself back again*. This means placing yourself at God's disposal to do anything and everything He will ever ask you to do. And if you will do that, you will always be in a position to hear what God has to say to you, and God *will* speak to you because you have become a surrendered living sacrifice.

STUDY QUESTIONS

Study to shew thyself approved unto God, a workman that needeth not to be ashamed, rightly dividing the word of truth. — 2 Timothy 2:15

1. Read John 16:13. Put this verse into your own words. What does this mean about your future?

2. Is there a time in your life you can recall laying down what you wanted to do for God's plan? What was the result?

PRACTICAL APPLICATION

But be ye doers of the word, and not hearers only, deceiving your own selves. — James 1:22

1. Take a moment to examine your heart. Ask God if there are any areas in your life that are not aligned with His. Record those areas. Purpose

to lay down your life, your will, to do His will and to follow His plan for your life.

2. What is the dominating voice in your life at this time? If it is not God's voice, God's Word, or God's Spirit, are you ready to release your own plans and surrender your will to His?

TOPIC

What Does 'Holy and Acceptable Unto God' Mean?

SCRIPTURES

1. **Matthew 16:25** — For whosoever will save his life shall lose it: and whosoever will lose his life for my sake shall find it.

2. **Romans 12:1** — I beseech you therefore, brethren, by the mercies of God, that ye present your bodies a living sacrifice, holy, acceptable unto God, which is your reasonable service.

3. **Luke 2:22** — And when the days of her purification according to the law of Moses were accomplished, they brought him to Jerusalem, to present him to the Lord.

4. **1 Corinthians 6:19** — What? know ye not that your body is the temple of the Holy Ghost which is in you, which ye have of God, and ye are not your own?

5. **1 Thessalonians 4:4** — That every one of you should know how to possess his vessel in sanctification and honor.

6. **Deuteronomy 6:5** — And thou shalt love the Lord thy God with all thine heart, and with all thy mind, and with all thy might.

7. **Romans 6:13** — Neither yield ye your members as instruments of unrighteousness unto sin: but yield yourselves unto God, as those that are alive from the dead, and your members as instruments of righteousness unto God.

GREEK WORDS

1. "beseech" — **παρακαλέω** (*parakaleo*): to urge, beseech, plead, beg, pray; pictures someone who has come closely alongside another person for the sake of speaking to him, consoling him, comforting him, or assisting him with instruction, counsel, or advice; depicts military leaders who came alongside their troops to urge, exhort, beseech, beg, and plead with them to stand tall and face their battles bravely; to earnestly beg; denotes a word of prayer

2. "mercies" — **οἰκτιρμός** (*oiktirmos*): tender feelings; compassion; a divine power released to help us

3. "present" — **παρίστημι** (*paristemi*): to place at one's disposal; to surrender; to offer as a sacrifice to God; to present as a special offering to God; to dedicate; used in Luke 2:22 to describe the moment when Joseph and Mary presented Jesus to God and dedicated Him in the Temple; to fully dedicate with no intention of ever taking back again

4. "instruments" — **ὅπλα** (*hopla*): a tool; a weapon

5. "unrighteousness" — **ἀδικία** (*adikia*): unrighteousness; injustice; hurt

6. "yield" — **παρίστημι** (*paristemi*): to place at one's disposal; to surrender; to offer as a sacrifice to God; to present as a special offering to God; to dedicate; used in Luke 2:22 to describe the moment when Joseph and Mary presented Jesus to God and dedicated Him in the Temple; to fully dedicate with no intention of ever taking back again

7. "instruments" — **ὅπλα** (*hopla*): a tool; a weapon

8. "unrighteousness" — **ἀδικία** (*adikia*): unrighteousness; injustice; hurt

9. "living" — **ζάω** (*zao*): to be living; lively; vibrant

10. "sacrifice" — **θύω** (*thuo*): to sacrifice; originally referred to the sacrificial slaughter of animals on the altar; to surrender; to give up something that is precious and dear

SYNOPSIS

In Romans 12:1, Paul says, "I beseech you therefore, brethren, by the mercies of God that you present your bodies a living sacrifice, holy, acceptable unto God, which is your reasonable service." What does it mean when the Bible says "holy, acceptable and reasonable service"? One thing is sure, you will never get to verse 2 until you do verse 1. Verse 2 is where we find the will of God, but you can't get to verse 2 until you first present yourself *a living sacrifice, holy, acceptable unto God.* That is the subject of this lesson.

The emphasis of this lesson:

In today's lesson we will examine what the Bible means by presenting our lives as *a living sacrifice*. Exactly what does that mean and how will we accomplish it? That is the focus of this lesson.

The will of God really is the key to having a successful life. What does the Bible mean when it says we are to present ourselves as a living sacrifice? Before we continue in Romans 12:1, I want to look at Matthew 16:25 where the Lord Jesus uttered these marvelous words: "For whosoever will save his life shall lose it: and whosoever will lose his life for my sake shall find it."

Paraphrased, this verse reads, **"Whoever wants to cling to his own plans, cling to his own life, and do it the way he wants to do it will lose a lot in life. But if anyone is winning to lose his life or sacrifice his life for My sake, he will really find what his life is all about."**

Those are powerful words! Rick said in this program, "I am a living testimony that when I surrendered to the will of God, my life literally became vibrant. It was like I stepped out of a black-and-white world into full color. My life had already been pretty good, but when I really laid my own plans aside and said, 'God, I'm going to come into alignment with Your plan — I'm going to live to do Your will; that is why I'm here," that is when the adventure really began!

God has an equally exciting plan for you! You are not here by accident. Jesus said, "…Lo, I come (in the volume of the book it is written of me,) to do thy will, O God" (Hebrews 10:7). You can say that to the Lord too!

Every Purpose Under Heaven

Ecclesiastes 3:1 clearly says, "To every thing there is a season, and a time to *every purpose under heaven*."

You are under the heavens, so that means there is a purpose for you. Ephesians, Chapter 1 says, before God ever laid the first crust of the earth, He already had designed a plan specifically for you. God has been waiting a long time for you to surrender and step into His plan. That is when life will really begin to make sense. Jesus said, "If you lose your life for My sake, you will really find what your life is all about." It is understandable that it can be a struggle to lay aside your own plans to embrace the will of God. But not only is it possible, it is what God requires.

Coming Alongside

We began examining Romans 12:1 in the last lesson. It is a fabulous verse concerning knowing God's explicit will for our lives.

I beseech you therefore, brethren, by the mercies of God, that ye present your bodies a living sacrifice, holy, acceptable unto God, which is your reasonable service.

Re-examining the word "beseech" in this verse, it is the Greek word *parakaleo*. The Greek word *para* means *to be alongside*. This indicates Paul is drawing close to his reader. The Greek word *kaleo* means *to call out*, so Paul is coming alongside and speaking to us with a tender heart. Paul is really calling out to us. The Greek word *parkaleo* could be translated *to urge*. It could also be translated *to plead* or *to beg*. In fact, as discovered in our last lesson, it is a word for *prayer*. Some expositors say this is a picture of the great, legendary apostle Paul dropping to his knees. While on his knees, he is literally pleading with and begging you and me.

But this Greek word *parakaleo* was also a military term, which is very important in the context of this verse. This word depicted military leaders who came alongside their troops just before they went into battle to urge them, exhort them, beseech, beg, and plead with them to stand tall, throw their shoulders back, and face their battle bravely.

Warfare of the Mind:
The Battle in Our Wills

First, Paul was begging. He was pleading, on his knees, praying that we would hear what he was about to say. Secondly, he understood what he was about to tell us to do would thrust us into warfare with our mind, with our flesh, and with our will. Paul knew that in order for us to win this battle, it would be necessary for us to stand tall, throw our shoulders back, and be brave. We would need to bravely charge into the fray, ultimately defeating our will and our flesh.

In the last lesson, we saw that Jesus had to deal with this in the garden of Gethsemane. The Bible tells us Jesus was in agony when He was in the garden because the will of God was leading Him to the cross and to the grave. But His mind, His will, did not want to go there. That is the reason Jesus prayed three times, "Not *My* will, but *Thy* will be done." It was a battle in His will. And the Greek word for the agony Jesus experienced in the garden — *agonia* — pictures two wrestlers slugging it out on the mat. Jesus was literally in a wrestling match as His heart led Him to the will of God at the same moment His flesh was saying, *"No, no, no!"* and His mind was also screaming, *"Don't do it!"*

But as we know, Jesus won the battle because He surrendered in the garden of Gethsemane. In fact, the real victory for our salvation was not won at the cross — it was won in the garden of Gethsemane when Jesus completely surrendered to the Father's own plan.

It is possible to defeat the battle in your mind and in your emotions. Paul said, "I beseech you and I plead with you by the mercies of God." The word "mercies" is the Greek word *oiktirmos*, which describes tender mercies and a compassionate feeling. But in Greek it describes *a divine power that is released to help us.* That means that God's power and mercy are available to help us present our bodies as a living sacrifice. If we will make the decision to present ourselves, God's mercy will be activated, enabling us to carry this out.

Placing Yourself at God's Disposal

The word "present" is the Greek word *paristemi.* It is a very important word. It means *to place at one's disposal.* So if you are going to *present yourself as a living sacrifice,* you are placing yourself at God's disposal.

As mentioned in the previous lesson, the same word is used in Luke 2:22, speaking of Joseph and Mary obeying the Law of Moses as they took Jesus to Jerusalem "to *present* him to the Lord."

Luke 2:22 says, "And when the days of her purification according to the Law of Moses were accomplished, they brought him to Jerusalem, to *present* him to the Lord...."That word "present" is the same word found in Romans 12:1. It means *to fully dedicate with no intention of ever taking back again.* There was a onetime presentation dedicating Jesus completely to the purposes of God. Paul used the same word in Romans 12:1, meaning we are to officially dedicate ourselves to the Lord, once and for all, to the plans and the purposes of God.

Have you ever finally surrendered yourself to the plans and purposes of God? To really know the will of God for your life, you must surrender your life completely to Him.

Total Surrender — Mind, Will, Emotions, and Body

Paul continued in Romans 12:1, "I beseech you therefore brethren by the mercies of God that you present your bodies." In this particular instance, the word *body* includes our entire being. It would include our mind, our will, our emotions, and our body — everything about us and everything we are. Think about this: Is your body yours or the Lord's? Have you ever officially said, "Lord, I'm giving you my body"? You may say, "Well, I gave my heart to Jesus." That is vital, but after salvation, have you ever given Him your body?

Your Body Belongs to God

In First Corinthians 6:19, Paul stated, "What? Know ye not that your body is the temple of the Holy Ghost which is in you, which ye have of God, and ye are not your own?" Your body belongs to Jesus. In First Thessalonians 4:4, the apostle Paul says, "…Every one of you should know how to possess his vessel (body) in sanctification and honour…."

You possess your body — you live in and steward it — but it belongs to God. In this verse, Paul is referring to "body *management*." Our body really does not belong to us; it belongs to the Lord. Our responsibility is to manage and take care of our body to ensure it remains a vessel or an instrument for the Lord. One way to discover whether or not you have dedicated your body to the Lord is very simple. Look in the mirror and ask yourself if you look like someone who has presented his body to the Lord. If you look in the mirror and realize by looking at the image staring back, "I'm not taking care of my body. I'm not eating right. I'm not doing right with my body," chances are you have never really officially dedicated your body to the Lord.

You Mind Belongs to God

How about your mind? Who does it belong to? Deuteronomy 6:5 says, "And thou shalt love the Lord thy God with all thine heart, and with all thy soul (mind), and with all thy might…."

Have you ever officially presented your mind to the Lord, once and for all, never to take it back again? If you have never surrendered your mind to Christ, then it is likely you are not really living under the full lordship of Christ because the mind is the central control center for your life.

Whoever controls your mind controls you. That is why the devil so desperately wants your mind. Whoever controls your mind controls you — what you think and what you feel. When Jesus is Lord of your mind, He really has you. He has access to all of you. Have you ever presented your mind officially, once and for all — never taking it back again — to the plans and purposes of God?

Your Emotions Belong to God

Emotions are powerful; they were created by God. When emotions are operating in a person who is controlled by the Holy Spirit, emotions can become a powerful weapon. But if emotions are in your own grip — unpresented to the Lord — they can be destructive, manipulative, and controlling. Emotions can hurl you into a mess.

Who controls *your* emotions? Have you ever officially dedicated them to God once and for all? Maybe you say, "This is one area of my life that is mine. I have a right to feel what I want to feel!"

But do you really? Is that really going to serve you well in life and promote the plans and purposes of God where you're concerned? If you are committed to the lordship of Jesus, you give up your rights to just feel "any old way."

Have you ever surrendered your emotions to the Lord, or are your emotions in your own grip?

Become a Weapon of Righteousness — *Not* a Weapon of Hurt and Injustice!

In Romans 6:13, the apostle Paul made an important statement: "Neither yield ye your members as instruments of unrighteousness unto sin: but yield yourselves unto God, as those that are alive from the dead, and your members [your body] as instruments of righteousness unto God."

The word "instruments" is the Greek word *hoplon*. It is the word to describe *a tool or a weapon*. It is the same word used to describe the weapons found in Ephesians 6. A better translation of this verse would be as follows: "Neither yield your members as weapons of unrighteousness." The word unrighteousness is the Greek word *adikia*, which means, *unrighteousness, injustice, or hurt*.

If you have never really surrendered yourself to the Lord, you may have become a weapon of injustice — a weapon that causes hurt in the lives of other people. Let me ask again: Who do you belong to? Are you in your own hands or are you in the hands of the Lord? That is the reason Paul continued, "…But yield yourselves unto God." The word "yield" is the Greek word *paristemi*, the same word that is translated "present" in Romans 12:1.

In the past, you might have been a weapon of injustice, a weapon that caused hurt in the lives of other people, but if you will surrender yourself to the Lord, everything can change. You can become a weapon of righteousness. The word "righteousness" is the Greek word *dikaiosune,* which means, *justice, rightness, or righteousness.* God can bring justice through you. You can become a weapon God uses. You can become a mighty weapon in the hands of God if you will *paristemi* — present yourself to the Lord once and for all, permanently, never taking yourself back again.

Romans 12:1 again says we are to present our bodies as "a living sacrifice," not a dead sacrifice. This word "living" is a form of the Greek word *zao,* which describes something *living, lively, or vibrant.* The word *sacrifice* is translated from the word *thuo,* which means *to sacrifice.* But originally, it referred to the sacrificial slaughter of animals on an altar. It meant *to surrender or to give up something that is precious and dear.*

Pagan Sacrificial Practices

Paul was writing the people in Rome. These were pagans who had grown up committing pagan sacrifices. To understand what Paul was saying, we must understand the anatomy of a sacrifice. Sacrificing to the gods in the pagan world was a very important event in a person's life. It was festive, it was public, and it was very celebrated. In addition to the public sacrifice, there were also smaller, private sacrifices conducted in the home to reconfirm the public sacrifice made earlier. So there were large public sacrifices and then smaller daily sacrifices in the confines of the home that were private and that reaffirmed the earlier sacrifices made publicly.

The animals to be sacrificed were decorated, their horns were painted, and all types of wine and barley were thrown over the back of the animal. The animal would then be marched into the temple and up the steps to the altar. The animal's throat was then cut on the altar, and as the blood poured out, it was collected and poured out onto the fire. The sacrificed animal was then cut into pieces and the pieces burned until the animal was completely consumed. There was no such thing as a living sacrifice. It did not exist. Death and blood were required for sacrifice — or it was not a sacrifice. If a person walked away with a living animal, then no sacrifice had been made. It was not official unless something died. That is very important to understand.

A Living Sacrifice

Paul instructed us in Romans 12:1 to offer our bodies, our minds, our emotions — everything we are — as *a living sacrifice*. As in all sacrifices, death is required. In this case, it is not *physical* death, but a death to our own will — a death to *ourselves* — a surrendering of ourselves to the plans and purposes of God. It should be a celebrated moment in your life, presenting yourself with great joy to the Lord: "Here I am to do Thy will, O God."

We are to be *living sacrifices*. The word "living" implies this is not a onetime sacrifice. Perhaps you have already made a public commitment of your life to the Lord, but every day, you need to privately reaffirm that commitment in your private prayer, saying, "Lord, here I am. I'm surrendering my life today. I am Yours. Everything I am — my mind, my will, my emotions, and my body — everything that I am. I am presenting myself to You as a living sacrifice." We must give our lives, once and for all, and we must never take them back again. We must die to our own will and plans. If there has been no death, there has been no sacrifice. And though you make this commitment "once and for all," it's okay to confirm and affirm and reaffirm it often in your walk with the Lord.

God calls on us to present all of us — every part of us — as a living sacrifice. And as in all sacrifices, if there is not a death, there has been no sacrifice. Something has to die. In this particular case, God is in no way requiring physical death, but He is calling on us to forfeit our will, to lay our own plans aside, and to crawl up on the altar of God every day, if needed, and say, "God here I am. I give myself to You. I am here for Your plans and Your purposes."

When you make that kind of commitment, that is when you become an acceptable offering unto God, and God will begin revealing His plan for your life.

STUDY QUESTIONS

Study to shew thyself approved unto God, a workman that needeth
not to be ashamed, rightly dividing the word of truth.
— 2 Timothy 2:15

1. Read Acts 9:1-31 about Saul's conversion. What as the result of Paul's surrendering his life to God's plan?

2. According to this passage in Acts 9, explain why you believe Paul really understood Romans 12:1 when he wrote, "I beseech you" — *parakaleo.*

3. Read Philippians 3:3-9. List two areas in which Paul laid down in his life to surrender to God. What have you laid down? List two areas.

PRACTICAL APPLICATION

But be ye doers of the word, and not hearers only,
deceiving your own selves.
— James 1:22

1. Set apart time before you start your day to present yourself a living sacrifice. Ask the Lord if there is any area you need to lay on the altar today. Completely surrender and make note of how your day went compared to days when you did not surrender your life.

LESSON 3

TOPIC

What Is Real Inward and Outward Transformation?

SCRIPTURES

1. **Romans 12:1** — I beseech you therefore, brethren, by the mercies of God, that ye present your bodies a living sacrifice, holy, acceptable unto God, which is your reasonable service.

2. **Joshua 24:15** — Choose ye this day whom ye will serve.

GREEK WORDS

1. "beseech" — **παρακαλέω** (*parakaleo*): to urge, beseech, plead, beg, pray; pictures someone who has come closely alongside another person for the sake of speaking to him, consoling him, comforting him, or assisting him with instruction, counsel, or advice; depicts military leaders who came alongside their troops to urge, exhort, beseech, beg, and plead with them to stand tall and face their battles bravely; to earnestly beg; denotes a word of prayer

2. "present" — **παρίστημι** (*paristemi*): to place at one's disposal; to surrender; to offer as a sacrifice to God; to present as a special offering to God; to dedicate; used in Luke 2:22 to describe the moment when Joseph and Mary presented Jesus to God and dedicated Him in the Temple; to fully dedicate with no intention of ever taking back again

3. "living" — **ζάω** (*zao*): to be living; lively; vibrant

4. "sacrifice" — **θύω** (*thuo*): to sacrifice; originally referred to the sacrificial slaughter of animals on the altar; to surrender; to give up something that is precious and dear

5. "holy" — **ἅγιος** (hagios): holy; consecrated; different; separate

6. "acceptable" — **εὐάρεστος** (*euarestos*): from **εὖ** (*eu*) and **ἀρέσκω** (*aresko*); the word **εὖ** (*eu*) means well, well done, swell, good, correct, or right; the word **ἀρέσκω** (*aresko*) carries the ideas of delight, joy, or something that is virtuous; compounded, the new word portrays something that is exceedingly pleasing and pleasurable; something that is way over the top in terms of the pleasure it brings; depicts a sacrifice that is fully pleasing; an event that brings God pleasure

7. "reasonable service" — **λογικὴν λατρείαν** (*logiken latreian*): from **λογικός** (*logikos*) and **λατρεία** (*latreia*); the word **λογικός** (*logikos*) means rational, logical, or that which agrees with reason; the word **λατρεία** (*latreia*) depicts priestly ministry and all the services rendered by those in the priesthood; this phrase depicts the rational, logical, and expected service that should be provided by anyone in the priesthood; hence, the anticipated and expected behavior of any believer who has yielded himself as a living sacrifice; logical priestly function; a full-time function; a life-long occupation

SYNOPSIS

We are continuing our study on knowing the will of God. When you find the will of God, you suddenly wake up. You will feel like you have stepped into a full-color spectrum of your life. You will step out of a black-and-white world into a full-color world! God wants you to step into the most marvelous, adventure-filled life; He is simply waiting for you to get your mind renewed and for you to surrender yourself so you can discover His plan for your life.

The emphasis of this lesson:

In today's lesson, we will focus on how to prepare our minds to hear the perfect will of God for our lives.

Lay It All Aside

Just as we have learned in the first two lessons, you will never know the will of God until you lay aside your own will. As long as your own will is in the picture, the waters are going to be muddied and it will be very difficult for you to hear what God really wants you to do. I completely understand this, because I have had moments in my life when I had to lay aside my own will so I could hear what God had to say. God wants to speak clearly to us, but if we have our own ideas, our own will, or our own plans, it becomes difficult for us to hear the will of God. We must be willing to lay it all aside and say, "God, my ears are open to hear whatever You have to say to me and I have a heart to obey."

If we have a heart to obey and if we are willing to hear, God will speak to us and reveal His plan to us for our life. He will reveal His plan for our marriage, our finances, what church to attend, what job we ought to have, and what we are to do in ministry.

Some people say, "God works in strange and mysterious ways." Not really. If you study Scripture, you'll find that God is very habitual in the way He works. If we just clear our mind to hear and allow the will of God, the voice of God, and Scripture to be the dominant voice in our life — above our opinions, our ideas, and our feelings — we will hear God speak to us and He will reveal His plan to us.

Romans 12:1 and 2 are probably the best verses in the New Testament about knowing the will of God. In today's lesson, we will focus on completing verse 1, which says, "I beseech you therefore, brethren, by the mercies of God, that ye present your bodies a living sacrifice, holy, acceptable unto God, which is your reasonable service."

Present Your Body a Living Sacrifice

In this verse, Paul is about to ask us to do something that may thrust us into warfare. He will ask us to *present* our bodies, our minds, our emotions — everything we are — as *a living sacrifice*. When we begin the process of presenting ourselves as a living sacrifice, to hear and do the will of God, our flesh sometimes argues. Our will struggles.

But Paul says we must face this battle bravely. Presenting our bodies can thrust us into spiritual warfare. We must throw our shoulders back, hold our head high, and determine we will win this battle.

Public Commitment — Private Affirmation

We learned in the last program concerning "the anatomy of a sacrifice" that if there was no death, there was no sacrifice. Death and blood were required for a sacrifice. It was not a true sacrifice unless something died. This was all included in this Greek word "sacrifice," or *thuo*. By using this word, Paul tells us we are to be living sacrifices. We are to present ourselves to the Lord publicly and it is to be celebrated, to be festive, as we also learned in the last program. This should be a grand occasion in our lives when we celebrate the giving of ourselves to God. But then on a daily basis, in the privacy of our prayer time, we need to reaffirm to the Lord, "Here I am, reconfirming that I have given myself to You." So we have an initial public giving and a private daily reaffirmation.

God calls us "once and for all" and also daily to surrender ourselves to His plans and His purposes. Once we have become a living sacrifice, we can never take our lives back into our own hands. Again, if there has been no death, there has been no sacrifice. And it is certainly not calling for physical death, but He *is* calling us to die to ourselves.

Acceptable to God

Jesus told us in Matthew 16:25, "For whosoever will save his life shall lose it: and whosoever will lose his life for my sake shall find it." We lose our life by surrendering ourselves to the plans and purposes of God. The word "holy" is a translation of the Greek word *hagios*. This word *hagios* is a primary word for the word *holy* in the entire Bible. The word *hagios* describes *something that is holy, consecrated, different, separated, or consecrated*.

Again, Romans 12:1 says, "…That ye present your bodies a living sacrifice, holy, acceptable unto God, which is your reasonable service." When we present ourselves to the Lord, He says, "That is a special, holy, consecrated act." Suddenly, we place ourselves in an entirely different category. There are believers who are surrendered, and there are believers who are *not* surrendered. There are many believers living for themselves — for their own plans and ideas — but when you surrender yourself fully to the plan of God and determine to never take yourself back into your own hands again, suddenly you enter into a new category. This is holy and consecrated. In fact, as Paul wrote, it is *acceptable unto God*.

The word "acceptable" is the Greek word *euarestos*. It is a compound of the Greek words *eu* and *aresko*. The word *eu* describes *something that is well, something that is done well, or something that is good, correct or right*. The word *aresko* carries the idea of *delight, something that is filled with joy, something that is virtuous*. When the two words are compounded, the new word portrays something that is *exceedingly pleasing and pleasurable, or something that is way over the top in terms of the pleasure it brings*. It depicts *a sacrifice that is fully pleasing* or *an event that brings God pleasure*.

When we really present ourselves to the Lord, it brings great delight to the Lord.

Our Reasonable Service

"Reasonable service" is a Greek phrase *logiken latreian* from the Greek words *logikos* and *latreia*. The word *logikos* is where we get the word *reason or logic*. The word *latreia* is the word for *the priesthood*. The word *logikos* means *rational, logically or that which agrees with reason*. The word *latreia*, the second part of this phrase, depicts *priestly ministry and all the services rendered by those who are in the priesthood*. This phrase together depicts *the rational, logical, expected service that should be provided by anyone in the priesthood*. Thus, it is the anticipated and expected behavior of any believer who has yielded himself as a living sacrifice. This "reasonable service" is a logical priestly function — a full-time function and lifelong occupation.

Paul said this is the kind of priesthood that God expects you to live in and to perform. And it is logical and reasonable. After all that God has done for you — after Jesus shed His blood so that God could extend redemption and forgiveness to you, give you gift of the Holy Spirit and the Word of God, and pour out all grace upon your life — "reasonable service" is expected of any believer who claims that he has surrendered himself. This is his logical and lifelong occupation — to live as a sacrifice, pleasing unto God.

Choose Whom You Will Serve

All of us will serve somebody. You will either serve yourself or somebody else. You will serve sin or your will serve righteousness. You will serve God or you will serve another.

That is why Joshua 24:15 says, "Choose you this day whom you will serve." You are going to serve somebody, so you might as well choose to serve God with your life. As long as you are struggling to have your own way, it will be very difficult for you to ever find the will and plan of God. As long as you have your own plans, you probably won't find God's plan.

Your plan and God's plan may or may not be the same, but you will never know unless you surrender your plans and open your ears and say, "God, here I am. I am presenting myself, *paristemi*. I am officially placing myself at Your disposal. I am making a once-and-for-all dedication, never taking myself back again. I am a living sacrifice, crawling up on the altar and dying to any of my own plans and ideas. I am surrendering myself fully to You."

God says, "Presenting yourself as a living sacrifice is holy, awesome, special, well-pleasing, and brings Me incredible delight." Paul says it is your reasonable service as a priest, as one redeemed; it is what God *expects* of you. God is expecting us to live as surrendered people for the rest of our lives. It is truly our *reasonable service.*

STUDY QUESTIONS

Study to shew thyself approved unto God, a workman that needeth not to be ashamed, rightly dividing the word of truth. — 2 Timothy 2:15

1. Read Exodus 2:1-10, the story of Moses' birth. How do you think Moses' mother laid it all aside to do God's will? What was the result of her being willing to die to her own desires?

2. What have you laid aside for God that turned out so much better because of your surrender to Him?

PRACTICAL APPLICATION

But be ye doers of the word, and not hearers only, deceiving your own selves.
—James 1:22

1. Take time to examine your heart. Is there an area in your life you have been unwilling to surrender to God? If so, why have you been unwilling? Or perhaps you have struggled in the past to lay down your plan, perhaps in a relationship or a job or another area. Reflect on your struggles in the past to surrender to God. How did you overcome that struggle? What was the result of laying down your will for God's plan?

LESSON 4

TOPIC

What Is the 'Good, Acceptable, and Perfect Will of God'?

SCRIPTURES

1. **Romans 12:1-2** — I beseech you therefore, brethren, by the mercies of God, that ye present your bodies a living sacrifice, holy, acceptable unto God, which is your reasonable service. And be not conformed to this world: but be ye transformed by the renewing of your mind, that ye may prove what is that good, and acceptable, and perfect, will of God.

2. **Romans 12:1 (RIV)** — Do not pattern your thinking after the way the world system thinks…

3. **Ephesians 2:2** — Wherein in time past ye walked according to the course of this world, according to the prince of the power of the air, the spirit that now worketh in the children of disobedience.

4. **James 2:21** — Was not Abraham our father justified by works, when he had offered Issac his son upon the altar?

GREEK WORDS

1. "conformed" — **συσχηματίζω** (*suschematidzo*): to pattern or to fashion oneself according to another

2. "world" — **αἰῶνος** (*aionos*): age; in this context, it describes the fluctuating tides of thinking in the world system

3. "according to" — **κατά** (*kata*): according to; carries the idea of domination

4. "transformed" — **μεταμορφόω** (*metamorphoo*): the word **μετά** (*meta*) and **μορφόω** (*morphoo*); the word **μετά** (*meta*) means a turn or a change; the word **μορφόω** (*morphoo*) depicts a shape, form, or essence; to change or to turn into a new shape, form, or essence; in this verse, pictures a mind that is in in the process of transformation

5. "renewing" — **ἀνακαίνωσις** (*anakainosis*) the act of making new again; to put back into its original condition before it was spoiled; to renovate; a complete renewal or restoration

6. "good" — **ἀγαθός** (*agathos*): anything good, beneficial, or profitable

7. "acceptable" — **εὐάρεστος** (*euarestos*): from **εὖ** (*eu*) and **ἀρέσκω** (*aresko*); the word **εὖ** (eu) means well, well done, swell, good, correct, or right; the word **ἀρέσκω** (*aresko*) carries the ideas of delight, joy, or something that is virtuous; compounded, the new word portrays something that is exceedingly pleasing and pleasurable; something that is way over the top in terms of the pleasure it brings; depicts a sacrifice that is fully pleasing; an event that brings God pleasure

8. "perfect" — **τέλειος** (*teleios*): pictures a full-grown adult; the process of transitioning from being youthful and immature to full-grown and mature; in the New Testament, it denotes spiritually mature individuals who are living in accordance with the will of God

SYNOPSIS

In Romans 12:2, the Bible says there is a "good, acceptable and perfect will of God." Most Bible believing Christians want to know, "God, what is Your will for my life? What is Your plan for me?" It is important to understand, you don't need to take a shot in the dark and hope you are headed in the right direction. To do so is a waste of time, energy, and money. God does not want you to waste anything. It is His desire to reveal to you His good, perfect and acceptable will. How do you determine if you are in the will of God? What are the signs?

The emphasis of this lesson:

In this lesson, we will identify those signs to help you determine where you stand in God's plan for your life.

If We Give God Our Mind, He Will Give Us His Will

In today's lesson, we will continue our study of Romans 12:1,2: "I beseech you therefore, brethren, by the mercies of God, that ye present your bodies a living sacrifice, holy, acceptable unto God, which is your reasonable service. And be not conformed to this world: but be ye transformed by the renewing of your mind, that ye may prove what is that good, acceptable, and perfect, will of God."

If you want to know the perfect will of God for your life — to know what is that *good, acceptable, and perfect will of God* — you must do the first part of the verse, which says, "…And do not be conformed to this world, but be ye transformed by the renewing of your mind." **If we give God our mind, He will give us His will.** This verse says *be not conformed to this world.* The word "conformed" means *to pattern or to fashion oneself according to another*, which is a reference to the world. The word "world" is really the Greek word *aionos.* The use of the word "world" in this passage is not a good translation. It more accurately means *the age* or *the current trends.* This verse would be more accurately translated, "*Do not pattern your thinking after the way of the world system and its thinking.*"

Example of World System Thinking

Morals:

Morals fluctuate in society. What was once morally unacceptable can become acceptable. People frequently change their moral standards. If you fashion your thinking according to the morals of the world, the foundation is not solid.

Psychology:

It seems about every ten years, modern psychology reviews what has been previously taught and practiced and then seems to revise everything. If you base all of your beliefs according to modern psychology, it is an unstable foundation, because its standards fluctuate.

Diet:

How about diet? Nutritionists and doctors seem to constantly change dietary standards. One year, chocolate is bad for your health. The next year it is considered healthy. One year, coffee is unacceptable for a healthy lifestyle, but the next year it is considered beneficial. If you are building your belief system for your life according to what nutritionists and doctors say, it is not a steady foundation.

Philosophy or Entertainment:

What about philosophy or entertainment? Philosophies and entertainment are ever-changing. They function according to the whims of the times — whatever is the newest trend, the most cutting-edge idea. The areas of philosophy and entertainment are continually fluctuating. This portion of Romans 12:2 could be translated, "Do not pattern your thinking after the way the world system thinks."

A Biblical Worldview

In my book *How To Keep Your Head on Straight in a World Gone Crazy*, I give two worldviews: 1) a *biblical worldview* and 2) a *non-biblical worldview*. A biblical worldview is based on the infallible Word of God. When a person adheres to the view that the Bible is entirely true, he consequently allows it to be the foundation of everything he says and does. This is my personal position and from this position, I will never deviate. Decades from now, I will continue holding to this position, because my faith is deeply rooted in the unchanging voice of Scripture.

Those who have a *non*-biblical worldview will fluctuate on many issues that are already answered for those with a biblical worldview. Even the most basic issues for this group shifts because their beliefs are affected by the ever-changing current thought and by the most recently accepted norms, whatever they may be at any given moment. A non-biblical worldview is primarily fashioned and informed by the fields of science, medicine, and education as well as societal norms. These factors are constantly in a state of flux created by variant shifts in society and most current acceptable theories and cultural norms. Those who adopt this view will likely change what they believe multiple times in the years to come. This is an unstable and unreliable path that floats on trends rather than on faith, which is fixed in absolute truth.

According to the Course of This World

If you are fashioning your thinking and believing according to the *aionos*, or age, you're in trouble because you do not have a strong or solid foundation. You are on a foundation that is adrift and constantly fluctuating. But if your beliefs are based on the Bible, your beliefs will not change because you're standing on a solid foundation. The apostle Paul refers to this in Ephesians 2:2. He says, speaking of unbelievers, "Wherein in times past ye walked according to the course of this world, according to the prince of the power of the air, the spirit that now worketh in the children of disobedience."

The verse begins with, "Wherein in times past...." This is a description of Paul's audience before they came to Christ. The Greek really means, "Back then, before you came to Christ, back then when you walked according to the course of this world." The word "walked" is the Greek word *peripateo*, which describes a lifestyle of *habitually walking around*.

The phrase "according to" is the Greek word *kata*. It carries the idea of *domination*. This could be translated, "You walked around, living your lifestyle, being dominated by the course of this world." Even the word "world" here is very important. It is the Greek word *kosmos*, which carries the idea of *culture, society, fashion, trends, what is currently popular but may not be popular tomorrow — the course of this world*. All of these trends are fluctuating, blowing in and blowing out. Here we have a picture of people fashioning themselves according to trends rather than according to truth. This is the most unstable, unreliable path for a person to take in life.

The Prince of the Power of the Air

In Ephesians 2:2, Paul continues, "...According to the prince of the power of the air." As mentioned previously, what is vital to understand is the phrase "according to" in Greek is the word *kata*, meaning *being dominated by the prince of the power of the air*. This reveals that all the trends, fashion, secular education, and what Hollywood purports to be true and fashionable is all just a façade; working behind it all is the prince of the power of the air. If you are fashioning your thinking according to trends and what is popular, the standard you have chosen is ever-fluctuating, very temporal, and extremely unsteady. Working behind it is *the prince of the power of the air* who is manipulating people and society like puppets. Both unbelievers and Christians who live according to the world's standards end up being mental puppets. They are constantly being manipulated, changing their thoughts according to whatever society says is acceptable or what they read on social media. By these standards, there is no stability in their lives. But those who live according to the Word of God live by an unchanging standard that is constant. It never changes.

A Transformed Mind

God's will for us is to be permanently transformed in our thinking through a greater understanding of what the Bible says. The Bible is not optional; it is the authoritative voice of God, our daily bread. By reading and believing the Bible, Romans 12:2 says your thinking will be *transformed*. The reason we should want our thinking transformed is so we can prove what is that *good, acceptable and perfect will of God*. We have a responsibility in the transformation of our mind. Just because you are saved does not mean you have a transformed mind.

What does it mean to have a mind that is transformed? The word "transformed" is from the very same Greek word used in Matthew 17 to describe the Mount of Transfiguration. To have a *transformed* mind is to have a *transfigured* mind. It is comprised of two Greek words. *Meta* carries the idea of *a change* — and *morphoo* depicts *a shape, a form, or an essence*. When these two words are compounded, the new words means *to change or to turn into a new shape, to turn into a new form, to give it a new essence*. This verse depicts *a mind that is in the process of transformation* or *transfiguration*. Again, it is the very same word used in Matthew 17 to depict the Mount of Transfiguration when Jesus' form was literally transformed as witnessed by Peter, James, and John.

In the same way, our minds can be transformed, our minds can be transfigured. In fact, the Bible tells us to "be transformed by the renewing of our mind." The word "renewed" is also very important. It is the Greek word *anakainosis*. It is a compound word comprised of *ana* and *kainoses*. The word *ana* means *to do it again* — and the word *kainosis*, from the word *kainos*, means *new*. Together the meaning is *to make new again, to put back into its original condition before it was spoiled, or to renovate; a complete renewal or restoration.*

Rick related the following illustration to further make that point.

> I think about an apartment our family purchased when we first moved to the Soviet Union. It was a large apartment that at one time had been lovely. But by the time we purchased it, it was completely dilapidated. Eight families had lived in this one apartment; it had been a communal apartment from the Soviet days. There was one toilet, and men had missed the toilet so many times, urine had eaten a hole all the way through the floor. We could literally look through this hole in the bathroom floor down to the floor below us. All of the windows in the apartment had been knocked out; mold was growing and graffiti was written on the wall. Plastic was stretched across one room to keep the plaster from falling onto the floor. It was a horrible, horrible mess and in extremely poor condition.
>
> Little by little, we began to renew that apartment. We renewed the walls, put in new windows, installed new plumbing, and got rid of the mold. We restored all of the previously magnificent molding in the apartment that had been obscured by 55 years of paint. By the time we had finished, we had totally renovated that apartment. We restored it to its original condition. The truth of the matter is it was in even better condition than when it was first constructed.

According to Paul's words in Romans 12:2, if you will put the Word of God into your mind, your mind will be transformed. In fact, your mind will be so transformed, it will be returned to the condition God originally intended.

An Investment Into Your Mind

Just as it took the Renner family time to renovate that apartment, it will take time to be transformed in your mind. To renovate your mind, you must be very intentional. It is an investment. It will take effort. It will take energy. It will take a commitment. Just as the Renners were committed to renewing that apartment and worked on it day after day until it was finally restored, you will need to be committed and determined to renew your mind. You must be resolute about restoring and renovating your mind and replacing wrong thinking by renewing your mind to the truth. You must make a conclusive decision — that the Bible is the final authority in your life. The Bible must be the dominating voice that speaks into your life. You need to come to a moment of mental surrender.

All believers must come to a place of mental surrender to the fact that the will of God is found in the Bible. You must decisively, authoritatively, and infallibly decide that no voice has more authority in your life than the Word of God because the Word of God contains the will of God.

In the Bible, the will of God for every situation in this life is addressed, either in fact or in principle. Some people by their actions think they are smarter than the Bible, but time always proves that the Bible is absolutely accurate. We need to embrace it, and if we embrace the Word of God, it will save us.

Receive the Engrafted Word

You may wonder, what does that mean? James 1:21 explains: "Wherefore lay apart all filthiness and superfluity of naughtiness, and receive with meekness the engrafted word…."

The "engrafted word" refers to the Bible. The reason it is *engrafted* is because it is not original to you. You have to *receive it*. If we will make room for the Word of God in our heart and mind and receive the engrafted word, James describes the result — *it is able to save our soul.*

The word "save" is the Greek word *sozo*, meaning *to save, to heal, to deliver, or to preserve.* The word "souls" is the Greek word *psuche*. It describes *the mind, the will, and the emotions.* In other words, when you fill your mind with the engrafted word, you allow it in and make room for it, it will begin to take root in your heart and mind and literally begin to release its delivering power, its healing power, its restorative power in your mind, will, and emotions. Your mind is transfigured, renewed, and begins to think on a higher level, and it is easier for you to perceive the voice of God and know God's plan for your life.

Rick said in the program that he remembered a time in his life when he was really determined to renew his mind and he literally inundated his mind with God's Word. He pressed so hard into Scriptures, he could feel molecules moving in his brain; it was literally being subjugated to the power of the Word of God.

Even scientists tell us that the mind has plasticity and can be reshaped. It can be renewed. If you will inundate your mind with the Bible, it will renew your mind, your mind will be transformed. When the mind is transformed, knowing the will of God is really not so difficult — for example, what job to take, who to marry, who not to marry, all those areas become very elementary decisions when your mind has been renewed. The renewed mind is able to easily grasp and see clearly areas previously difficult for you to see and hard for you to understand.

Even a damaged mind can be repaired. It can be reshaped and miraculously renewed if it is regularly filled with the truth, believes the truth, and puts the truth into action. This won't happen without a determined purpose to do so, but for those who make the effort, this activity will reshape and reform the mind, freeing it from damage and restoring it to be the mind God originally intended for it to be. That is amazing!

Proving the Good, Acceptable, and Perfect Will of God

Romans 12:2 says if we will do this, we will be able to prove what is that *good and acceptable and perfect will of God*. The word "good" is the Greek word *agathos* describing *anything good, beneficial or profitable*. The word "acceptable" is a Greek word *euarestos*, portraying *something that is absolutely wonderful, exceedingly pleasing, and pleasurable; something that is way over the top in terms of the pleasure it brings*. The word *perfect* is the Greek word *teleios* describing *a full-grown adult*; it pictures *the process of transitioning from being youthful and immature to an adult who is full-grown and mature*. In the *New Testament*, it denotes spiritually mature individuals who are living in accordance with the will of God.

Rick said that when he was young, it was difficult for him to grasp the will of God, but as he delved into the Bible to renew his mind and began to "bombard" his mind with the right information from the Word of God, his mind began to sharpen; it began to be fine-tuned so the things that were once so difficult for him to understand became very easy to grasp. And things that were once difficult became simple.

The same will happen for you if you will simply bombard your mind with God's Word. Your mind will be transformed, renewed, and you will easily understand what is the good, acceptable and perfect will of God for your life. But you must be willing to make the investment to do it. You must choose to put time and effort into it. That is the reason Romans 12:2 says you must present yourself as a living sacrifice once and for all, never reneging on the commitment, determined not to quit — and to surrender all of yourself, including your mind, to the transforming power of the Word of God. If you will do that, things that once evaded you and seemed so difficult to understand, you will easily begin to see and understand because the molecules of your mind will begin to work differently, having been transfigured by the power of God's Word.

STUDY QUESTIONS

Study to shew thyself approved unto God, a workman that needeth not to be ashamed, rightly dividing the word of truth.
— 2 Timothy 2:15

1. Are there areas in your life where you have conformed to the world's thinking because of current societal "norms"? Perhaps it has been a gradual shift. If such an area exists in your life, find a scripture that contradicts that wrong thinking.
2. Are there any areas in your life that feel unstable? Identify those areas. Find one verse that will bring stability to each of those areas in your life.

PRACTICAL APPLICATION

But be ye doers of the word, and not hearers only, deceiving your own selves.
— James 1:22

1. Think about your worldview. Identify two areas that are biblical. Write a scripture supporting that view.
2. If there is an area or areas where you have drifted into an unbiblical worldview, identify that. Think about why your view is not biblical. Find one verse to renew your mind in that area(s).

TOPIC

Six Signals To Know the Will of God

SCRIPTURES

1. **2 Corinthians 13:1** — In the mouth of two or three witnesses shall every word be established.

2. **1 John 5:14-15** — And this is the confidence that we have in him, that, if we ask any thing according to his will (the Bible), he heareth us: And if we know that he hear us, whatsoever we ask, we know that we have the petitions that we desired of him.

3. **Romans 8:14** — For as many as are led by the Spirit of God, they are the sons of God.

4. **Psalm 37:4** — Delight thyself also in the Lord; and he shall give thee the desires of thine heart.

5. **Psalm 20:4** — May God grant your heart's desires and make all your plans succeed.

6. **Romans 14:23** — …for whatsoever is not of faith is sin.

7. **Hebrews 11:6** — …And without faith it is impossible to please him…

GREEK WORDS

1. "led" — **ἄγω** (*ago*): to lead: often depicted animals led by a rope tied around their necks and that followed wherever their owner led them; thus, to be led; the owner would "tug" and "pull," and the animal followed

SYNOPSIS

Did you know God has a plan for you? You're not an accident. The Bible tells us in Ecclesiastes 3:1, "To everything that is under the heaven there is a purpose." If you are under the heaven, this verse means you are not an accident, you were not a last-minute thought. God had a plan for you before the foundation of the world. In fact, Ephesians 1:4 says, "According as he hath chosen us in Him before the foundation of the world, that we should be holy and without blame before Him in love." God has been waiting a long time for you to show up so He can reveal His power and His glory through you. You may be wondering, *Well, what is the plan and what are the signs to let me know I'm on track?*

The emphasis of this lesson:

Today's lesson covers six concrete signs to determine if you are in line with God's plan for your life. God has a plan and He is not trying to hide it from you. These six signals will help you determine if you are aligned with God's will and plan for your life.

In the Mouth of Two or Three Witnesses

In today's lesson we are going to identify six signals indicating what is or is not the will of God for your life. In Second Corinthians 13:1, the apostle Paul shares a very important principle when he says, "In the mouth of two or three witnesses shall every word be established." According to Paul, when God is saying something, He confirms it in the mouth of two or three witnesses. This principle also applies to knowing the will of God. If God is revealing His plan to you, He will confirm it in the mouth of two or three witnesses. He may confirm it through the mouth of your pastor, through a circumstance, or you may be reading the Bible and, suddenly, a verse speaks to your heart. When God is telling you to do something, He will confirm it in the mouth of two or three witnesses. When He does that, it gives you a very firm foundation to stand on. If there are multiple witnesses confirming something in your life, it is like a green light. If there are conflicting signs, it is like a yellow traffic light and you should slow down. And if you see several signals that say, "No, don't do this," you need to take it as a red light and proceed no further.

When the six signals covered in this lesson line up, you have a green light. If a few of these say, "No," then you need to move with caution. But if several of them say "no," then you need to take it as a red light and you need to stop the direction you are headed.

Six Signals

Number One: *The Voice of the Bible*

God will never ask you to do something contrary to His Word. The God who is leading you is the same God who inspired the Bible, and He will never lead you to do things contradictory to what He has clearly stated in the Bible. Anything that is contradictory to what is taught in the Bible will never be the will of God. For example, adultery is never the will of God. God is not leading you to a new relationship if it is adultery. Stealing is never the will of God; you don't even need to pray about that. That is contradictory to the teaching of Scripture. Lying is never the will of God; being disrespectful to authority is never the will of God. You cannot excuse those behaviors or even convince yourself that maybe, somehow, in some way, in this particular case, God is making an exception, because it would be contradictory to what God has already spoken in His holy Word. The God who inspired the Bible will never lead you to do something that is contradictory to the teachings of the Bible. God's revealed will is found in His Word. That is why it is so important for you to read the Bible. If you don't have a daily reading guide, contact RENNER Ministries, and we will help you get one.

In First John, 5:14 and 15, the Bible says, "And this is the confidence that we have in him, that, if we ask any thing according to his will [that's the Bible], he heareth us; And if we know that he hear us, whatsoever we ask, we know that we have the petitions that we desired of him."

When we stick with the Bible, we are on safe ground because the Bible reveals the will of God. For example, healing is the will of God. That is found in the Bible. Walking in integrity is always the will of God. That is what the Bible says. Tithing is the will of God. That is what the Bible says. Not committing adultery — it is the will of God for you to walk in marital integrity. That is what the Bible says. There are some issues so clearly stated you don't even need to pray about them because the Bible clearly addresses them. The God who is leading you is the same God who inspired the Bible, and He will not lead you to do things contradictory to what He has clearly stated in the Bible.

Number Two: *The Voice of the Holy Spirit*

If we will listen, the Holy Spirit will lead us. In fact, we are promised in Romans 8:14, "…As many as are led by the Spirit of God, they are the sons of God." This means if we are children of God, we have a right to be led by the Holy Spirit. The word "led" is the Greek word *ago*. It means *to lead*, but it often depicted *animals led by a rope, tied around their necks who followed wherever their owner led them; the owner would tug and pull and the animal would follow.* This is the picture of the Holy Spirit leading us. He will tug and pull on our hearts. This verse says that if we are children of God, we need to expect the Holy Spirit to lead us.

Number Three: *The Voice of Your Own Heart*

You must learn to listen to your heart because God gives you desires. God will give you the desires of your heart because God put those desires in your heart. He did not give you desires that are contrary to the teaching of the Bible, but He did give you desires. For example, maybe you have a desire to sing or a desire to do business that burns inside your heart, and you are constantly praying, "God, please show me your will." Yet all the while, God's will is exploding inside you; you simply need to listen because God puts desires in your heart.

Psalm 37:4 says, "Delight thyself also in the Lord: and he shall give thee the desires of thine heart."

Psalm 20:4 (*NLT*) says, "May he grant your heart's desires and make all your plans succeed."

Number Four: *The Voice of Spiritual Leaders*

Older leaders who know us very well can help us discern the will of God for our life. Rick remembers when he and Denise were first married. Rick had wanted to purchase an old house, a house that had actually been burned down, but it was an old Civil War home in the city where they lived, and he wanted to renovate that house. He had always had a desire to renovate homes or to upgrade property. So he began working on that house when an older seasoned leader said to him, "Rick, what in the world are you doing?"

Rick related:

> At first it offended me because I thought he just didn't have the vision and didn't understand my desire. But he said, "Rick, let's really walk through this. Would God really lead you to do something like this when you don't have the money for this project? You have no available resources to turn to. You may start this project, but you won't be able to finish it. You will end up with a real problem." After he pointed out the pitfalls, I understood at that early age in my life that I was just excited about having a project, but it was not wise or practical. That older man spoke

such wisdom to me, but I had to be willing to listen; I had to be willing to submit.

Another example of a voice that spoke wisdom into Rick's life that made a great difference was Pastor Bob Yandian. Pastor Bob heard Rick teach a series and approached him saying, "Rick, this series is so significant — I think you ought to put it into a book." At the time Rick hadn't attempted to write a book in years, because years before, he had tried to write a book and someone ridiculed him about it, which discouraged him. But when Bob Yandian said to Rick, "I believe God wants you to put this message into a book," Rick respected him so much that he took his counsel very seriously. As a result of the pastor's advice, Rick began to write his first book. And the reason Rick writes books today is because Bob Yandian spoke to him and told him he needed to begin writing. God used an older, seasoned leader to speak into Rick's life.

We need to listen to the voice of the Bible, we need to listen to the voice of the Holy Spirit, we need to listen to the voice of our own heart, and we need to listen to the voice of older, mature spiritual leaders who speak into our lives. That may be your parent, your pastor, a person who is disciplining you, or someone older than you in the Lord. Simply keep your ears open and have an open heart so they can speak into your life. God may speak to you through them. After all, God will confirm His will through two or three witnesses. He will speak through the voice of the Bible, He will speak through the voice of the Holy Spirit, He will speak through the voice of your own heart, and He will speak through the voice of seasoned, mature, spiritual leaders.

Number Five: *The Voice of Circumstances*

The lowest level of leading is God speaking through the voice of circumstances. You should not be led by circumstances, but neither should you ignore circumstances. You should pay attention to circumstances because often, when things line up, it is a "green light" or a confirmation that you are supposed to do something. And when doors close, very often it is a signal that you are headed in a wrong direction.

There was another instance early in Rick's life concerning something he wanted to do, and every door just slammed shut. He was so discouraged by that, and the Lord spoke to him and said, "Rick, very often a door will close before the right door will open. Never be discouraged by a door that closes."

So pay attention to circumstances, but don't be led by circumstances alone. This is a very low-level kind of leading. First, hear the voice of the Bible on the subject. Secondly, listen to the voice of the Holy Spirit. Third, listen to the voice of your own heart. For example, what is in your own heart, in your own soul? Does your heart beat for this?

Fourth, you need to listen to the voice of spiritual, seasoned, mature leaders. But, fifth, you also need to listen to the voice of circumstances. Are circumstances lining up or are the doors closing? Pay attention. Sometimes when it seems doors have closed, it is devilish opposition and you will need to resist it. Other times, it is God closing doors. That is the reason you need to listen to older, seasoned leaders. They will help you to discern God's will and plan.

Number Six: *The Voice of Faith*

This is very important. The Bible tells us in Romans 14:23, "…Whatsoever is not of faith is sin." In this program, Rick also shared: "I have learned through the years that when God is leading me to do something it usually will require me to increase my faith. If it is a true leading of the Lord, it means my faith will be challenged, my faith will be stretched, and I will be required to grow."

God is not only interested in using us — He wants to change us as He uses us. God wants us to go from strength to strength; He wants us to go from glory to glory, and when God asks you to do something, it will require faith. Listen for the voice of faith.

Think about Moses. When he led the children of Israel into the Promised Land, they had to go through the Red Sea and it required faith. When God told Joshua to lead the children of Israel across the Jordan River into the land of promise, they had to cross the Jordan at flood stage and it also required faith. For Jesus to come into the world to redeem you and me, it required faith.

Jesus said in Hebrews 10:7 (*NLT*), "I have come to do Your will, O God — as it is written about me in the Scriptures."

It required faith for Jesus to come into the world to die on the cross, believing what was spoken of Him in the Scriptures — that after the Cross, He would be resurrected. Faith was required for all of it. Furthermore, we are told in Hebrews 11:6, "But without faith it is impossible to please Him [God]."

In conclusion, when we are seeking God's will in specific areas of our lives, there are six voices that can confirm if we are aligned with His will.

Number One: *The Voice of God's Word*

The voice of God's Word must be in agreement.

Number Two: *The Voice of the Holy Spirit*

The voice of the Holy Spirit is tugging or pulling on your heart and leading you in a certain direction.

Number Three: *The Voice of Your Own Heart*

Don't ignore your own heart. God may have put certain desires in your heart that are the will of God for your life. Listen to your heart. God will give you the desires of your heart if those are desires that He has placed there.

Number Four: *The Voice of Spiritual Leaders*

Thank God for the voice of older, seasoned, mature spiritual leaders who speak into our lives. Even today, I listen to the voices of those who are older than me and are seasoned; their counsel is invaluable.

Number Five: *The Voice of Circumstances*

Rick summarized: "In my own life, whenever a great door opened for a particular TV channel we had been waiting for, if it suddenly all opened, but the other circumstances didn't line up and I didn't have the cash to pay for TV time, I had to discern whether or not that was actually the will of God. If I had a 'green light,' I would act."

Number Six: *The Voice of Faith*

This is when God asks you to do something that stretches your faith, like crossing the Red Sea or the Jordan River — something you could never do by your own skill, talents, intelligence, or strength. When you feel like you have a "green light," step out in faith!

When all of these voices line up, as Second Corinthians 13:1 says, "In the mouth of two or three witnesses shall every word be established," very likely, you have a "green light" — a confirmation from God. If several of these voices say "no," you need to proceed with caution, and if many of them say "no," you can interpret it as a "red light" and should wait on a decision.

It never hurts to wait, just to be sure you are aligned with God's plan. But if you have a "green light," don't hesitate — go forward! God is beckoning you through the door into His will, into His plan, and when you step through that door, you will leave a black-and-white world and step into a world of full color!

There is nothing more important than doing the will of God. Find it. Follow it. And let the adventure begin!

STUDY QUESTIONS

**Study to shew thyself approved unto God, a workman that needeth not to be ashamed, rightly dividing the word of truth.
— 2 Timothy 2:15**

1. List the Six Signals for determining if your plan is aligned with God's for your life in a particular area.
2. List one instance in which God confirmed His plan in your life for each of the Six Signals.
3. Read Acts 13:2. Describe how Paul and Barnabas could be certain they were walking in God's perfect plan for their lives.

PRACTICAL APPLICATION

**But be ye doers of the word, and not hearers only, deceiving your own selves.
— James 1:22**

1. Think of a time when you know you missed God's will in an area of your life. In retrospect, how did the Lord try to help you avoid getting off course? What did you learn from this experience?

Notes

Notes

_____

_____

_____

_____

_____

_____

_____

_____

_____

_____

_____

_____

_____

_____

_____

_____

_____

_____

_____

_____

_____

_____

_____

_____

_____

www.ingramcontent.com/pod-product-compliance
Lightning Source LLC
Chambersburg PA
CBHW071744020426
42331CB00008B/2176

Porque Eu Escrevi Este Livro

——————⟨⟩⧫○⧫⟨⟩——————

O Que Entra Em Você Determina O Que Existe Em Você.

Onde Deus está... satanás não está.

Quando Saul estava deprimido, os maus espíritos vieram de encontro à sua mente e ele mandou chamar o salmista Davi.

A bíblia diz que quando Davi começou a tocar a harpa, o espírito mau foi embora. Quando Davi começou a cantar, o Espírito Santo entrou e os maus espíritos se foram.

"Daí em diante, toda vez que o espírito mau mandado por Deus vinha sobre Saul, Davi pegava sua lira e tocava. O espírito mau saía de Saul, e ele se sentia melhor e ficava bom novamente", (1 Samuel 16:23).

Deus Não É Uma Presença... Ele É Uma Pessoa Com Uma Presença. Sua Presença É A Evidência de Sua Pessoa.

O *Grasnido* não é o *Pato.*

O *Latido* não é o *Cão.*

O Espírito Santo é uma Pessoa. Ele não é um *Fogo...* Ele *Purifica* como o fogo. Ele não é *Água...* Ele *Limpa* como a água. Ele não é um *Vento...* Ele se *Move* como o vento.

O Espírito Santo pode se mover repentinamente e de maneira rápida na sua vida, como o vento. "De repente, veio do céu um barulho que parecia o de um vento soprando muito forte e esse barulho encheu toda a casa onde estavam sentados", (Atos 2:2).

A Bíblia tem muito a dizer sobre Deus, a *Pessoa,*

A *Aura,* a *Presença* de Deus.

O Antigo Testamento é diferente do Novo Testamento. No Antigo Testamento o Espírito Santo *Visitou.* No novo testamento Ele *Permanece.* No Antigo Testamento os homens de repente *percebiam* ou *sentiam* a unção. Sanção experimentou isto.

Em certo momento da vida de Saulo ele se tornou muito diferente quando o Espírito Santo veio sobre ele que as pessoas perguntavam *"Ele é o mesmo homem?"*

No dia de Pentecostes, depois da ascensão de Jesus aos Céus, Ele disse: "Eu pedirei ao Pai, e Ele lhes dará outro Auxiliador, o Espírito da verdade, para ficar com vocês para sempre", (João 14:16).

Parece Haver Duas Imagens Distintas da Presença de Deus.

A Presença Universal de Deus se refere a onipresença do Deus que servimos.

O salmista se refere a isto, "Se eu subir ao céu, tu lá estás; se descer ao mundo dos mortos, lá estás também", (Salmos 139:8).

Jó disse: "Aonde posso ir a fim de escapar do Teu Espírito? Para onde posso fugir da Tua Presença?" (Salmos 139:7). "Estás em volta de mim, por todos os lados, e me proteges com o Teus poder", (Salmos 139:5).

A *Manifestação* da Presença de Deus acontece quando você percebe e sente Ele.

Há uma Escritura na Palavra que fala sobre Deus ser tão real que Sua presença *curou* muitas pessoas.

Isto parece indicar que há uma *Unção,* uma *Glória* e uma *Presença* que são diferentes em seus significados.

Ir a um restaurante, é diferente de quando você vai a um culto, aonde as pessoas cantam e adoram a Deus.